DARE TO SPEAK!

DARE TO SPEAK!

Discover the Secret of Successful Public Speaking

Frank Manfredi & Anthony Manfredi

authorHOUSE®

AuthorHouse™ LLC
1663 Liberty Drive
Bloomington, IN 47403
www.authorhouse.com
Phone: 1-800-839-8640

Published by AuthorHouse   06/25/2013

ISBN: 978-1-4817-6659-3 (sc)
ISBN: 978-1-4817-6658-6 (e)

Library of Congress Control Number: 2013911121

Contents

Introduction ix

Chapter 1   The Secret to a Powerful Speech 1
Chapter 2   A Quick History Lesson...6
Chapter 3   The Speaker...10
Chapter 4   Tools for the Speaker..16
Chapter 5   Should You Use PowerPoint?........................21
Chapter 6   Opening Thoughts on Writing
             Your Speech...28
Chapter 7   Grab Them from the Beginning...................31
Chapter 8   Your Message—Your Reason for Standing
             There 36
Chapter 9   More on Writing the Speech.........................42
Chapter 10   The Audience, Always the Audience...........51
Chapter 11   Wrapping It Up—The Close............................56
Chapter 12   Preparing for Delivery Day.............................58
Chapter 13   More Preparations for Performance..........64
Chapter 14   The Tools of the Trade.......................................70
Chapter 15   Speech Delivery Day!...74
Chapter 16   Video Conferences, Webcasts, and Other
             Technological Complications.........................76
Chapter 17   The Dreaded Meeting 82
Chapter 18   Modern Business Etiquette 90

Chapter 19   Are There Any Questions? 95
Conclusion   Dare to Speak!! 100

About the Authors..105
Bibliography..107
Endnotes...109

Dedication

This book is dedicated to the life and memory of
Josephine Manfredi, our family matriarch.
Now, there was a lady who never had a problem with
"Daring to Speak!"
She will be remembered and missed.

INTRODUCTION

Be sincere, be brief; be seated.
Franklin D. Roosevelt,
32nd President of the United States
(1882-1945)

Your name is called. It's time. You spring out of your chair and hustle to the front of the room where you survey your audience. Perhaps your gaze encounters only five members of your company, waiting to discover the details of your new program. Or you may behold an audience of 500 strangers, there to hear your keynote address.

Regardless of the size of the audience, *you* are now the center of attention. The pit of your stomach, which felt empty while you awaited your turn, has begun to churn. Your palms are sweating, your heart rate has increased, and your memory suddenly seems erratic. Within a few seconds, the murmuring of the audience fades and everyone is focused on you, the speaker. You can see anticipation and wanting in their eyes. "Entertain us, teach us, persuade us, show us," their eyes plead. You open your mouth to speak, and then . . . and then . . .

Countless books have been written on the subject of public speaking. Historically, we have Aristotle's *On Rhetoric,* and moving forward to 1926, Dale Carnegie's

Public Speaking: a Practical Course for Business Men. In fact, this resource remains the foundation of the Dale Carnegie Institute today.

In addition, Amazon.com lists more than 40,000 entries on the subject of public speaking—a testament to the ongoing revolution in the field of communication. Email has surrendered the main stage to Facebook, Twitter, and LinkedIn, and webcasts, podcasts, and videoconferencing abound. In most companies, not a single business day passes without the advent of several meetings that require speaking.

So why another book about public speaking? The answer is simple. Despite the volumes written to date and technological advances in the field, communication skills—especially in the business community—frankly stink.

One of the defining attributes of humankind is our ability to convey our thoughts to others. In fact, persuading and motivating others to act can be one of the highest callings if the ideas and thoughts conveyed are rational and beneficial. But how we waste these opportunities!

Suppose you have to give a 10-minute talk before 10 people and you blow it. Not only have you wasted *your* 10 minutes, but when you add up the time of the people in the room, you've also wasted 100 minutes of the audience members' time. That's nearly two hours down the drain.

We've likely all experienced sitting in a church, synagogue, mosque, or meeting place while the speaker drones on about some subject or another. Along with those around us, we shuffle, look at our watches, yawn. Our minds wander. At the end of the sermon, homily, or speech, we struggle to recall one salient fact or argument. Why? The speaker never reached us, never touched us either emotionally or intellectually. What a waste!

Yes, from the many books and courses on public speaking, you *can* learn how to write a speech or presentation and deliver it dynamically. But let me share with you a fact known to every speaker who has made a living giving talks. *You can deliver a speech or a presentation on a Monday to applause and cheers, then deliver the same talk or presentation two days later and get different audience results.* The substance of the talk was the same. Your delivery was just as polished on both occasions. What changed?

Many variables go into the preparation and delivery of a speech or presentation. Should you use PowerPoint—or not? What should you do with your hands? How should you use technological props? How should the room be set up? Where should you stand? Although you need to consider these factors, none of them are relevant to giving a speech that truly impresses your audience. Unless you learn the one true "secret" of effective public speaking, you won't be able to convey your message as well as you would like. As a result, your efforts may even be totally unconvincing.

On the other hand, you may mumble and stumble. Your computer and projection devices may crash, or the battery for your microphone may fail, yet you can still be an effective public speaker. Granted, it's preferable to speak properly and give a polished presentation, but these advantages merely augment the "secret."

Your speech might have the deep passion and exhortation of Pericles' Funeral Oration, the clarity and logic of Cicero's First Oration, or the crescendo and theatrics of Williams Jennings Bryant's Cross of Gold plea. Absent one essential ingredient, however, it will fall flat. Pericles, Cicero, and Bryant's speeches live on and continue to inspire students in classrooms today. Why? These speakers knew and incorporated the *secret ingredient*.

Chapter 1 reveals this key to effective public speaking. It lies in one simple word with French origins.

CHAPTER 1

THE Secret to a Powerful Speech

Nothing is so unbelievable that oratory
cannot make it acceptable.
Marcus Tullius Cicero, Roman author and
politician (106-43 B.C.)

In a memorable scene from the movie *A Time to Kill,* young attorney Jack Brigance, played by Matthew McConaughey, approached an all-white jury in a racially mixed Mississippi courtroom. His daunting—if not impossible—task was to argue for the acquittal of his client, a black man who had killed two white men.

As Brigance walked toward the jury, he faced their folded arms and sullen faces. Then he asked the jury members to close their eyes and picture the scene he was about to describe. Slowly, in vivid detail, he painted in their minds the rape and brutalization of the defendant's 10-year-old daughter by the two white men.

Suddenly pivoting in his presentation, Brigance said, "Now imagine that the little girl was white." His point seared through the jury. They wouldn't prosecute a *white* man who retaliated for acts of cruelty inflicted on his daughter. Shouldn't the same result apply to this *black* man, the defendant?

John Grisham, the author of the book this movie was based on, was well aware of the essence of successful argument. He knew the secret to public speaking. What might that be?

In a word, rapport.

This concept comes from the French word *rapport*, meaning connection or link. It occurs when a highly effective speaker or courtroom attorney establishes a meaningful connection or link with the audience. Dictionaries define the English word rapport as a close, harmonious relationship in which people or groups understand each other. Despite this simple definition, perhaps the most difficult task any speaker faces is to establish rapport.

In *A Time to Kill*, Brigance needed to persuade the jury to view the situation from a different vantage point. He accomplished that by telling the story in such a way that jury members would see the black man's humanity. He wanted to evoke compassion. Once he made that emotional connection, the logic in his presentation—namely, that there should be no difference between the treatment of a white father and a black father—was clear to the jury.

Whether you're speaking to throngs of people or only a handful, the principle is the same. Unless you learn how to use this key—rapport—your efforts to engage your audience and convey your message will fail more often than not.

Establishing a close understanding and relationship with an audience is an art, not a science. No formula exists for achieving it. However, this book explores tools you can use to help in this endeavor. As elusive as rapport can be, you know when you've achieved it and, as any speaker can attest, you also know when you haven't.

A work of fine art—a painting or a sculpture, for example—possesses a magical quality that can reach us on both emotional and intellectual levels. We can't always describe why we enjoy or connect with a painting. We might babble on about the color, the brushstrokes, or the depth of the artist's vision. But words alone can't do justice to the meaning the painting has for us. We've watched movies and found them unsatisfying. Why? Perhaps we can point to poor acting or a lousy plot, but often the movie just didn't "grab" us. It simply didn't hold our interest or move us. It lacked rapport.

In the art of public speaking, rapport holds a magical quality. But it's a quality that's difficult to attain because you're speaking to individual humans, and each person in the audience is different. Plus, each audience as a whole differs from place to place and time to time.

In addition, both individuals and audiences have their own sets of prejudices, biases, thoughts, beliefs, and agendas. Given that you, the speaker, want to penetrate their hearts and minds through your thoughts and emotions, don't expect to obtain rapport quickly. It's a subtle art! Attempt to make your listeners move *toward* you, emotionally and intellectually, knowing they're generally slow to do so.

Do you see why public speaking is tricky?

Frank Sinatra, one of the greatest entertainers of the 20th century, cultivated phrasing and lyrical control that became required study for any singer. But he possessed an even more important skill. Vocalists with better voices than his couldn't manage to achieve the "simpatico" relationship Sinatra developed with his audiences—the rapport. When he performed a ballad, his emotion was never overpowering. Rather, it emerged slowly from the lyrics, moving the audience to savor every nuance. A professor extraordinaire of rapport, Sinatra captured the hearts of his audiences for decades.

Abraham Lincoln had just finished his Gettysburg Address, his words lasting for only two minutes. His address contained a mere 10 sentences. At the end, silence filled the air, punctuated with only a few claps of polite applause. As he sat down, President Lincoln purportedly told his bodyguard that the speech was like an old plow and "won't scour." He thought he had failed. But I suggest the silence of the crowd was shock over the brilliant message he'd just delivered. Sometimes silence reveals the best example of rapport.

Let's review Jack Brigance's summation with the concept of rapport in mind. What did he do to create an atmosphere in which the jury would think about what he was saying and then act *favorably* on his argument?

First, he approached the jury with an air of humility and sincerity. *The speaker was authentic and truthful.* He spoke quietly and waited for jury members to focus on him. (I suppose if we all looked like Matthew McConaughey, it would be easy for the audience to focus on us. But most of us are ordinary looking, which is another reason rapport is difficult to achieve.)

Second, Brigance asked jury members to close their eyes. *The speaker achieved action from the audience that created a bond, a closeness.* Next, he recounted the crime against the young girl. *The speaker told a story.* Finally, he pivoted and changed the color, the race, of the victim. *Drama!*

In this one speech, the speaker created an aura of authenticity. He closed with his audience members by getting them to shut their eyes. Then he applied classic storytelling and, at the right moment, he startled them with a dramatic technique.

Authenticity, storytelling, bonding with the audience, and drama are but a few of the techniques that build rapport. And they only worked for Brigance because *he knew his audience!* and was able to create that magical feeling of rapport.

Chapter 2 looks back in time to see how the art of speaking has evolved. It notes a particular aspect of effective communication that seems to have gotten lost over the ages but remains essential to gaining rapport.

CHAPTER 2

A Quick History Lesson

Rhetoric is the art of ruling the minds of men.
Plato, Greek philosopher (428 B.C.-348 B.C.)

I plead guilty to being a history buff. I believe you never know who you are or where you are unless you know who you were and where you came from. The sad state of public discourse and public speaking is a case in point. It derives from the checkered past of the art form's origins, which are embodied in one word—*rhetoric*. Let's go back in history.

More than 500 years B.C. in the city-state of Athens, Greece, one of the first forms of democracy developed. Athenian democracy was a direct variety in that individual citizens voted on each law or position. Obviously, that form of democracy was cumbersome. It eventually evolved to our current style of government in the United States—namely, representative democracy—in which we elect representatives to vote on the various issues of the time. But in Athens, citizens had the solemn duty to participate; so to educate them on the problems facing the community, it was essential for knowledgeable people to speak in the various centers.

Thus, a group of itinerant intellectuals called Sophists arose. Traveling from one part of the city-state to another, these scholars taught oratorical skills, often for substantial fees. Their purpose was to reach a state of excellence or virtue through persuasive speech. Sophist teachings focused on techniques of presenting persuasive arguments. These techniques included poetry, philosophy, and figures of speech and the teachings became the foundation for the study of rhetoric.

Ironically, however, the Sophist approach created a moral problem. Sophists believed that, with proper training, a person could argue either side of an issue and, according to individual talent and ability, could be persuasive enough to win the argument. Because they were paid for their services—some quite handsomely—they tended to take the side of whoever paid them the most. Thus, truth easily became a casualty in this approach.

In today's society, the profession that most resembles that of the Sophist is the trial attorney—a verbal gunslinger who, for a fee, will argue for a client even if the client is guilty. One day a trial attorney may represent the plaintiff in a negligence suit and the next represent an insurance carrier in a malpractice case. Only the naïve believe that truth is always the outcome when two trial attorneys battle it out in a courtroom. Just like their Sophist predecessors, trial attorneys often use their rhetorical skills for self-advancement without regard to the truth of the matter at hand.

Enter Socrates, a teacher of public speaking without fee. Known as the Father of Western Philosophy, Socrates's questioning of the rich and powerful (now known as the Socratic method of arriving at the truth) caused embarrassment to many. Eventually, he was charged with impiety (questioning the gods) and corrupting the youth of Athens (with his teachings). He ended his life by his own hand, drinking poisonous hemlock. As far as we know, Socrates never wrote any texts, but his teachings were recorded by his student Plato.

For Plato, truth was of paramount importance—and could not be obtained by the Sophists and their methods. Hence, he turned his back on the concept of rhetoric as a useful tool. In its place, Plato opted for the dialectic—questioning by reasoned arguments—as the means to determine the truth or falsity of a position.

Why bring up philosophical methods of argument that occurred so long ago? The answer lies in Plato's grip on Western thought. Plato was the student of Socrates and no doubt blamed the Sophists for the death of his teacher. Echoes of his attacks on that group of supposed intellectuals reverberate in our language today. We define *sophistry,* a word derived from the Sophists of ancient Athens, as a subtle, tricky, superficially plausible but fallacious argument. And the study of persuasion through oratory (rhetoric)—once a great art form—now carries negative connotations. The word *rhetoric* is normally used with modifiers, such as classifying an argument as "merely rhetoric" or "empty rhetoric."

Plato was right. Truth is the essential goal of persuasion. Undoubtedly, the Sophists went astray. However, the criticism of rhetoric as a tool of persuasion was too severe, a fact noted by Plato's student Aristotle. In his textbook *On Rhetoric,* a work still studied today, Aristotle attempts to resurrect rhetoric as a vital tool for persuasion.

Today, public discourse and public speaking does not incorporate the revelation of truth sought by Plato. Too often, in fact, speakers use "spin" to hide reality. Their underlying agendas take precedence over thoughtful debate.

Truth is not easy. It requires an examination of opposing positions. In my opinion, you cannot take one position without acknowledging at least the existence of opposing positions. The solution is to merge the rhetoric with the truth. A youthful expression often heard on the streets is this: "He's keeping it real." Simply stated, for us, it means keep our words real.

So, to effectively "win over" an audience with your message, it's important to emotionally and intellectually touch your listeners—the essence of rapport. And for any attempt at rapport to succeed, you must be authentic and sincere as you follow Plato's advice: Speak the truth!

Any successful talk involves (1) the speaker, (2) the content of the talk itself, and (3) the audience. Of course all three are necessary and vital. Next, we'll delve into the first element of this triad, the speaker.

CHAPTER 3

The Speaker

All the great speakers were
bad speakers at first.
Ralph Waldo Emerson, American author and
philosopher (1803-1882)

At first glance, it appears that the speaker, talk, and audience are distinct aspects of a presentation and can be studied separately, but this isn't the case. The artistry of public speaking, the "magic," requires that all three elements intertwine to achieve maximum rapport between the speaker and the audience. Only then can a talk be considered successful.

Remember, as you speak, you're creating a work of art. As in a painting, all the elements must enhance the final image. Color, perspective, and subject matter become essential elements. With improper treatment of any one element, the painting becomes flat, absent of depth and feeling. The same is true with the essential elements of public speaking.

Let's consider the first element—you, the speaker.

A successful public speaker recognizes one fact: All speech is persuasion. Even your most mundane communication such as a quick "good morning" seeks to achieve a result, be it a smile or a verbal response in return. You're attempting to create connection, to persuade the other person to be friendly and warm as well. Your expression is more than politeness. Every word that comes from your lips has a message, a purpose. In a presentation or speech, your words are more formal but still, the purpose is to create connection.

The next few chapters discuss the preparation of your talk and the honing of your message, but suffice it to say it's important to communicate a clear purpose to your audience. Perhaps you've been asked to deliver a presentation explaining the results of the past quarter, so your purpose is to *educate*. But you're also trying to convince your colleagues intellectually and emotionally to understand what you're talking about, even *persuade* them to take action.

Your presentations may be about a new drug or a computer program, for example. You may want the audience to buy or recommend a product or become excited about a program. Therefore you're *persuading* audience members to do something. Occasionally, you may be required to deliver bad news to an audience. For that type of talk, you'd create an atmosphere in which you deliver the news and encourage action. Again, all speech is persuasion.

To start this process of moving people emotionally and intellectually toward your position, what attributes must you bring to the podium?

First, you must be authentic. So you don't set up a need to "fudge," be sure you know your material inside and out. Spend time to update your knowledge so you can present an air of authenticity. Audience members won't be moved to action unless they're convinced the speaker knows what he or she is talking about. That means conveying that knowledge in clear, concise, simple terms to meet their expectations.

Following our friend Plato's advice, be sure to speak the truth. While authenticity depends on having a firm knowledge of the subject matter, that becomes meaningless unless you can convey your message truthfully. If listeners believe you're conning them or spinning the message, they'll soon become deaf to it because they simply won't believe you.

Authenticity and truthfulness lead to the third element essential to the speaker—a combination of sincerity and humbleness that could be called sincere humility (as opposed to arrogance). Audiences see through phoniness. Unfortunately, when speakers have deep knowledge in a subject, listeners may perceive that they're pontificating, even talking down to them. While knowledge may produce authenticity and good character may engender truthfulness, humility and sincerity may not come easily to some—especially if they've had to *manufacture* a state of high confidence and a desire to impress their audience.

In 1995, famed trial attorney Gerry Spence wrote *How to Argue and Win Every Time*, a bible on the art of persuasion. Spence recognized the crucial nature of the relationship between speaker and listeners. To achieve this necessary bonding, the speaker demonstrates sincere humility by standing "naked" before the audience. Thankfully, Mr. Spence did not mean that literally! Rather, he meant that speakers must lay all their failings as well as the failings of their argument before the audience to evaluate.

Is there an argument that runs counter to your message? Then present it. Discuss it. Explain why this counter-argument isn't the correct way to go in this instance. Did you change your position on something? Let the audience know. Admitting problems and analyzing them before they're raised by your listeners demonstrates a kind of humility and sincerity; it shows you're "real." This humility serves as the basis for obtaining an emotional contact that leads to rapport.

The next step in creating rapport is to *empower* your audience members. You would *tell* them they have the power to accept or reject your position. Let them know you expect them to decide. That expectation brings people closer to the speaker rather than vice versa. It creates attention and makes them an essential element of the talk. In effect, they now have "skin in the game."

Both "standing naked" before the audience and empowering listeners to decide are essential to the humility and sincerity that create a bond between speaker and audience. A great example of the power of a speaker's authenticity, humility, and sincerity took place on April 4, 1968. Senator Robert F. Kennedy was campaigning for the Democratic nomination for president of the United States. As the candidate's plane landed in Indianapolis, the news media confirmed the death of Martin Luther King, Jr. by an assassin's bullet. Kennedy decided to keep his schedule and speak to the African American crowd that had been waiting for his appearance. Most of the throng knew nothing about the death of the civil rights leader. In one of his shortest speeches, Kennedy announced King's death and waited for the screams to die down. He talked about the death of his brother John, the former U.S. president who was assassinated. Then he closed his talk with a vision for an America based on love, compassion, and wisdom—instead of anger. Quietly, the crowd dispersed.

That night, anger raged in major U.S. cities and riots broke out across the country, but not in Indianapolis. Sadly, Robert F. Kennedy's life was also ended by an assassin just two months later.

Having suffered a personal loss by assassination made Senator Kennedy highly authentic in his Indianapolis speech. He presented the facts clearly and simply, and he was truthful. He stood in front of his audience with his own emotions revealed, and most important, he empowered the people. Specifically, he asked them to follow the road of compassion and wisdom rather than anger and hate. His short talk was humble and sincere. (For a video of this five-minute speech, go to www.youtube.com/watch?v=j6mxL2cqxrA;

the text of the speech can be found at www.historyplace. com/speeches/rfk-mlk.htm).

Although it's unlikely any of us will have to give a speech under such circumstances, Kennedy's presentation provides us with a worthy goal. He achieved total rapport with the audience that night. The substance of what he said contributed to his success, and so did his authenticity, truthfulness, sincerity, and humility. All these factors merged to achieve the ultimate goal of any speech: total rapport leading to successful persuasion.

CHAPTER 4

Tools for the Speaker

*If an eloquent speaker speaks not the truth, is
there a more horrid creature in creation?*
Thomas Carlyle, Scottish philosopher and
writer (1795-1881)

Most books on public speaking teach speakers to be themselves, stating no two speakers are alike in their presentation style. Some employ humor while others run from a laugh, fearing the attempt will fall flat. Some use stories to make a point and others consider them extraneous, preferring to stick to the core of their message. However, the purpose of all speakers is the same: to persuade and move the audience toward the speaker and the position presented. To achieve that goal, speakers must gain control of the room. To that end, certain techniques or tools have proven helpful, regardless of the speaker's style.

Tool #1: GAFTP

Your first tool is to simply Get Away From The Podium! You're asking those in the audience to "become one" with you by accepting your position, understanding it, even acting on it. So unless issues of national security or high diplomatic consequence require the precise reading of your speech—*move*. The podium or lectern creates a barrier between you and those in your audience. If you're on a stage, it's best to come out from behind it, walk the stage, and focus on sections of the audience as you go. Are their eyes following you? Are they paying attention? Do they "get" what you're saying?

If you're in a small group, walk among the participants. Get as close to them as you can without invading their space. Do they understand your message? Are the members of the group nodding in agreement on your point? Are they making sincere eye contact (not merely glassy eyes)? Do they appear to be thinking? If not, then clarify your point, change your approach, or (as a last resort) move on to another phase of your subject and later address any questions privately.

I acknowledge that staying behind a podium can serve as a crutch as well as a barrier. GAFTP assumes you know your speech (you'll find more on this subject as you continue reading). So if you need to, place your notes on the podium and occasionally wander over to peek at them, but then move around once again.

Tool #2: Eye Contact

A successful speaker is able to measure response from audience members largely through eye contact. Let your eyes move over the crowd and focus on a section. Are people following your movements? Are their heads moving up and down with approving nods? Are any participants shaking their heads negatively? Well, at least they're listening!

Be careful, though, not to make eye contact with one individual for an extended period or that person will become uncomfortable. As you move across the stage or floor, scan the sections. Check to see if you're reaching the audience. Their eyes will tell you.

Tool #3: Enthusiasm

Be enthusiastic about your presentation. With its roots in ancient Greece, the word *enthusiasm* means "being filled with God." Of course the meaning has changed since then, but for the speaker, it means being full of energy and passion. You can't expect people to embrace your position unless they believe you *care* about what you're saying.

Tool #4: Voice Modulation

Think of the voice—*your* voice—as the instrument you use to enthrall and captivate your audience. Modulate your tones from loud to soft at appropriate intervals to sync with the meaning of your words. Nothing puts the audience to sleep faster than a monotone presentation. If you write out your speech or presentation (discussed in Chapter 6), indicate the inflections you want on the paper—e.g., note which parts require loudness or softness. Plus, at times you may want to be quiet. Nothing creates drama or highlights an important point better than silence. Some call this tool the "pregnant pause." Done well, the silence drips with thoughtfulness or emotion. Modulation creates drama. Drama creates interest. Interest brings the audience closer to you, the speaker.

Tool #5: Pacing

The partner of modulation, pacing, means changing the speed of your speech at various intervals along with your voice level. So you would speed up when introducing a point and slow down when you get to the important part you want listeners to take away or the action you want them to take. When you change the pace, you also change your voice modulation, raising or lowering the sound and tone as you see fit.

You needn't join an actors' studio or become a Shakespearean expert, but make an effort to be *interesting* so you can achieve that magical moment of rapport. Get out from behind the podium, use proper eye contact, display sincere enthusiasm, modulate your voice, and vary your pacing. Then you're on your way to being a successful speaker.

Next, let's review a few tools you can use to enhance your presentation (if you wish), thanks to the latest computer technology.

CHAPTER 5

Should You Use PowerPoint?

I'm sorry, Dave, I'm afraid I can't do that.
Hal, the computer in *2001 Space Odyssey*
refusing a user request.

November 19, 1863. On the fields of Gettysburg, Pennsylvania, the 16th president of the United States is wrapping up his remarks. He turns away from the crowd and faces a white screen placed behind him by one of his staff. Clicking a button, he watches as the white screen instantly changes. A slide with bullet-points appears one line at a time:

Government . . .

- of the people
- by the people
- for the people

The president reads perhaps the most famous triplet ever created and then turns to the crowd, concluding with the words ". . . shall not perish from the earth."

Of course, I'm being facetious. Slides or no slides, President Lincoln was such a captivating orator that his speech would have been a success without using PowerPoint.

So why use slides? Because people process information differently. Some learn by listening (auditory), others learn primarily by seeing (visual), and still others learn and assimilate information by touching and manipulating (tactile, or kinesthetic). Slides can improve comprehension by appealing to those with a visual learning style.

Enter PowerPoint, a tool designed to augment presentations by requiring the audience to use the visual sense along with auditory processing. The theory appears sound, but taking that theory to reality in the sales room, auditorium, or conference hall may not be quite as easy or effective as it appears. Let's consider the problems involved.

Remember: PowerPoint and its counterparts (e.g., Google Docs, Apple's iWork, Slide Rocket, 280 Slides, and Prezi) can be helpful in *augmenting* your presentation—but never *supplanting* it. No amount of sound, pictures, video, or other "bling" will cure a poorly delivered message.

People often spend an inordinate amount of time creating the perfect slides for their presentation. I can only imagine the improvements they could make to their persuasive communication *if they devoted even a small portion of that time to honing their message*. Even a great PowerPoint presentation of moving slides and graphics won't save a presentation that's bereft of quality content and speaking skills.

Remember, when you stand before an audience, your purpose is to create rapport. Not only does using bullet points fail to accomplish this purpose, but it further distances you from those you want to persuade. That said, by all means prepare the slides to capture the important points of your presentation. Print them and hand them out at the end of your talk. Refer to them during a question and answer period, if you like.

But *during* your presentation, what is the most effective way to use PowerPoint? Let's see how an expert did it.

Steve Jobs demonstrated he was a master of graphics when he spoke. His presentations were dynamic and seamless. Screens were everywhere—on each side and behind him. When he used the printed word on a slide, often only one word would explode on the screen. That word indicated the subject of the next point of his talk. His colorful slides sported pictures and concepts. *Never did he permit the slides to divert attention from him or his message.*

Contrast Steve Jobs's style with the early slide presentations of Bill Gates. Gates's slides were cluttered with bullet points and detailed information. They required full concentration from the audience at the expense of the speaker.

In his recent presentations, Bill Gates's slides have become more dynamic, more closely mirroring the Jobs method of presentation. Comparisons of Steve Jobs and Bill Gates presentation slides abound. Just Google Steve Jobs v. Bill Gates presentation slides for ample examples.

A speaker is an artist. Whereas a painter has brushes and hues, speakers have words, yet both wish to create a picture for the audience.

Sometimes, however, words fail us as speakers and we find a picture truly is worth a thousand words. When I gave a speech on creative leadership, I was talking about the ability of a leader to change his goals quickly, depending on actual field conditions. In my preparations, I wanted to use as an example the leader of the Rangers who assaulted Point du Hoc during the D-Day invasion of Normandy on June 6, 1944. Intelligence reported that six large German cannons stood atop the cliff, ready to rain down destruction on the forces landing on Omaha and Utah beaches. Rudder's Rangers, led by LTC James Earl Rudder, scaled the cliff but, upon reaching the top, found no cannons. The radios were ineffective and time was short to communicate this fact. The Rangers regrouped and moved inland to find five of the cannons. They destroyed the cannons' mechanisms with thermite grenades.

In thinking about the situation, try as I might, I couldn't find the words to portray the heroic effort of these men. I decided that, when words fail, only a picture will do. So I created two slides depicting the height and danger involved in their feat, and these photos (two angles of the same cliff) drove home the message.

**Cliffs Scaled in the D-Day Invasion by
Rudder's Rangers, led by LTC James Earl Rudder**

**Cliffs Scaled in the D-Day Invasion by
Rudder's Rangers, led by LTC James Earl Rudder**

Seeing these pictures, the audience felt an emotional connection to the story. They could understand in a visceral way the challenge those men faced and conquered that June morning. This story demonstrates how PowerPoint can *supplement* a message, not divert attention from it.

You can achieve rapport by first securing an emotional tug, which permits the intellect to follow suit. Humor is one way to provide such a tug, and PowerPoint can assist in causing people to laugh, softening the crowd for the intellectual lift to follow.

For example, in a presentation I gave on "How to be a Project Manager," I used a blow-up Bozo the Clown doll decked out with a hard hat and contractor's vest. A paper sign taped to his chest identified the clown as a project manager. Placing the doll in various positions with the office staff and field personnel, I poked fun at myself and my position. My audience and I were able to turn to more serious matters quite quickly after the laughter subsided.

On another occasion, I was talking about "How to Conduct a Successful Meeting," and I borrowed a scene from *The Godfather*. If you saw that movie, you may remember the scene in which all the "dons" meet to negotiate a peace to the raging war. In the end, Don Corleone and Don Tattaglia saunter to the head of the table and embrace, sealing the peace.

Announcing with flair that I had a photo of what a successful meeting looks like, I showed a slide of that last scene. The embrace of these two characters stirred the room, breaking the emotional logjam.

PowerPoint is also valuable for presenting numbers, graphs, and charts. If used properly, this kind of slide can enhance the spoken word. It's one thing to announce to a group that sales have risen 10 percent over the first quarter. It's quite another to illustrate this showing a graph with an arrow rising upward. It gives your point a visual punch.

Simplicity, simplicity, simplicity is the key. Graphs must reinforce your point at a glance, with minimum explanation. Avoid cluttering the screen with columns of numbers.

Need help creating charts and graphs? The Internet is replete with advice. Your graphics can be picturesque, animated, or three-dimensional. But remember, "glitz" does not a presentation make. In fact, the message can become lost in the lights and whistles, so make sure you mainly focus on your message. Do you want your audience members to leave at the end of the presentation saying, "Those were great slides" or do you want them to say, "I understand what you were talking about"?

Probably you'd like to hear the best response of all: "I agree with what you said!"

CHAPTER 6

Opening Thoughts on Writing Your Speech

Give me six hours to chop down a tree, and I
would spend the first four sharpening the axe.
Abraham Lincoln, 16th president of the
United States (1809-1865)

Shortcuts in speech preparation simply don't exist. If you expected a quick guide that will make you an exciting speaker with a minimum of effort, you'll have to look elsewhere. Speeches are hard work.

First and foremost, everything you do as a public speaker must be audience-centered. Your knowledge of the potential audience feeds the creation of the speech and the eventual delivery of the talk. Let's assume you have to present disappointing sales figures that in turn will negatively affect year-end compensation for members of the audience. Your message is pointed—namely, that the company didn't meet its goals this past year and everyone in attendance will have to pay for it.

Would you write the same speech for an audience of grizzled construction workers counting on their year-end bonuses as you would for a group of computer programmers uncertain about the course of the company's IT investment? Or an audience of pharmaceutical executives concerned about pending federal regulations? No, you wouldn't.

The message is the same; the result (financial pain) is the same. But the audiences differ in terms of varied levels of financial acumen and education. Their industries are distinct, experiencing divergent economic directions.

Thus, I can offer no cookie-cutter recipes. Every talk must be different because, collectively, the people in the room are different. Ironically, there's no "right" or "wrong" way to prepare a talk. No two audiences are alike; no two speakers are alike; so no two talks can be alike. But take heart. Valuable keys do exist for organizing, preparing, and delivering a great speech or presentation.

Before delving into these keys, however, it's necessary to examine one paramount detail: your purpose. *Why are you talking?* Before sitting down to prepare your speech or write the first of many outlines (yes, many), you need to be clear about your message!

Write out your message in one sentence. For example, do you want your message to:

- tell your company about the vision for the upcoming year?
- explain new products that will be launched before the end of the year?

- provide the advantages of a new program that will save money for the business?
- delineate your position on a political problem?

These messages may seem simple to present. However, you'd be surprised how many times a speech wanders all over the place because the presenter has lost sight of the intended message. Your presentation needs cohesion and specificity. You have one talk, and it should present one message. Yes, of course you can use examples and details, but the entire speech should coalesce around *your one single message*.

Once you've expressed the purpose of your message in a simple sentence, turn to the other important aspect of any talk—the result. When the last word slips from your tongue, what do you want of your audience? What action, if any, do you want them to take? How do you want them to feel? What do you want them to think about?

A successful talk is measured by these two aspects: *Is the message clear and convincing? And did the audience receive it?*

Armed with knowing your message and the result you want from your listeners, let's move into Chapter 7 to begin speech preparation.

CHAPTER 7

Grab Them from the Beginning

Speak clearly, if you speak at all;
carve every word before you let it fall.
Oliver Wendell Holmes,
American jurist (1809-1894)

You may have only a minute or, at most, two. You have that short amount of time to set the tone for your entire presentation. It's your honeymoon period—the time when you have the audience's maximum attention. If you don't make the audience members your own by the end of the first two minutes, you may well spend the rest of your talk trying to capture their attention.

During these few moments as you open your presentation, you have much to accomplish. For this reason, it can be challenging to construct an opening. First, you want to set the tone of the talk. Will it be friendly and informal—or formal? Will it be light and fun—or serious and severe?

Next, within that short timeframe, you aim to create interest in your subject and build credibility with your audience—to initiate that feeling of rapport that builds and lasts throughout your talk. Then you segue smoothly into the body of your talk.

31

You can choose from several categories of openings. One type relies on **a question** such as:

- Is it possible to change our corporate culture?
- Can we turn around our dismal performance of the past quarter?
- Does a product exist that will save you money and make your work simpler?
- Is there a future for this type of product?

By posing a question, you gain your listeners' attention and control the tone. Yes, the question is rhetorical; no answer is required from the audience because in fact, your talk supplies the answer. Plus a question opening can pivot easily into the body of your talk.

Another type of opening involves the **use of quotations or other reference material** to enhance your position as a voice of authority**.** Referring to historical scenarios or a famous quotation lends gravitas to your presentation. In fact, you can refer to virtually *anything* including literary works, geography, history, personal experience, the previous speaker, the weather, or even comics. Still, your reference must have a point and segue into the body of your speech or presentation. An additional warning: You can choose from a virtually unlimited number of references for an opening, but make sure your audience knows what you're talking about. If I were speaking to a group of immigrants who recently received their citizenship, then talking about the heroic efforts of the 1969 New York Mets would miss the mark. However, I could discuss my grandfather's immigrant journey from Italy on the SS Taormina in 1927. That would be relevant and therefore enhance rapport with people in my audience.

Generally, question and reference openings are safe and easily meet the necessities of a good opening. Certain other openings may bring greater success but are fraught with peril.

First in this troublesome category is the **dramatic opening**, in which speakers use their voices and words to rouse great interest by creating a dramatic effect. Consider:

- I'm here today to announce an impending crisis in our company!
- By the end of the next decade, the way we do business will be extinct!
- We've been sitting on our past successes, resting on our laurels. Well, the past is *past.* We must change—and change *now!*

These dramatic statements are often preceded with a slight period of silence—the pregnant pause—a dramatic device used to gain attention. In addition, they're followed by silence to permit the drama to sink in. But this kind of opening is dangerous, for the drama must be real, and it must last throughout the speech.

When drama is used at the beginning of the speech to get people to rivet their focus on your message, you have to worry about fulfilling high expectations. Even the most dramatic scenes in a movie can't be sustained for long. In a movie, the director can cut to other facets of the plot—but not so in a speech. If the audience gets too riled up, it might feel a strong letdown. Thus, after the drama of the opening, take care to manage for disappointment with the message itself.

The **humorous opening** can be used to break the ice and is often an excellent step toward building rapport with the audience. But beware: Not everyone is a comedian. Should the humor fizzle or your timing be off, the entire speech might be doomed to failure because of a poor opening.

Note that the only type of humor to use in this situation is self-deprecating. That's right; make fun of yourself. By making a joke at your own expense, you ensure you won't offend anyone in your audience. And don't use canned jokes; the story about the traveling salesman is out. *Audiences want to laugh at the truth and humor they see in their everyday world.* So tell funny stories about your personal experiences. Oh yes—and don't laugh at your own stories. Let your listeners take it away. As the laughter subsides, you'll know when it's time to pivot to the main body of your speech.

Remember, prepare your opening from the *audience's* perspective. What works in front of one group won't work in front of another. Tailoring your opening to a specific audience means knowing as much as possible about that group of people, so do your homework.

The hard work continues as we turn to creating the body of the speech in Chapter 8. But keep in mind that working hard doesn't mean you can't enjoy the process—*and* focus on an excellent outcome.

CHAPTER 8

Your Message—Your Reason for Standing There

If you have an important point to make,
don't try to be subtle or clever.
Use the pile driver. Hit the point once.
Then come back and hit it again. Then hit it a
third time; a tremendous whack.
Winston Churchill,
British politician and author (1874-1965)

Your opening has been a success. You look at the people in your audience and they're paying attention. You feel them moving toward you. Now it's time to deliver the meat of your message, so you segue into the body of your talk.

As discussed, you already have two tools in your arsenal.

First, you've written out the theme, the purpose, the message you wish to convey, preferably in one short sentence. Remember—one talk, one message! Second, you have a firm grasp on the action you want the audience to take. It can run the gamut from learning, to buying, to selling, to changing, to even just agreeing with your message.

Before addressing the format of the talk, do your research. Even if you're well versed in your topic or have given the talk before, update your research material. With the state of knowledge constantly changing, there's nothing more embarrassing than having a listener challenge you on the facts. Start a research folder with the quotations and resource material you'll need for quick reference. The age of computers has made this much simpler, giving you access to fine research libraries on the Internet. Instead of the countless index cards once used to organize research material, you can now store it all for quick reference in folders on your computer's hard drive.

Next, sketch the body of your talk using the tried-and-true method of the outline. Whether you use your laptop, tablet, or handwritten notes on a yellow pad, you can't get away from it. You *must* outline.

That said, you needn't use the formal outline process taught in school or contained in the templates provided in your computer. A myriad of online outlining products are available. SplashNotes, OmniOutliner (Mac products), and Free Mind using mind-mapping techniques are only a few. Oh, and yes, pen and paper are still useful in this work. Survey respondents give this method an honorable mention. But however you do it, list each of the logical arguments that support your message, knowing it's best to limit these to three main points. Otherwise, you'll provide too much information and risk losing your audience.

Once you've listed the three main points, fill in the outline with facts you've accumulated through your research. You may choose to list an opposing position as one of the points in your argument, and then give facts to dispute that position. Once you've filled in your outline, organize all the information within the points, providing a semblance of order to the items if needed. Insert instructions in the outline such as which graphic you'll use when (if you decide to use slides).

As a hypothetical situation, assume you're the corporate safety director for a construction company that has suffered a rash of injuries over the last 18 months. Changes in the safety program are necessary, both for the welfare of your workers and the company's bottom line. You've been called on to address 30 project managers and announce these changes. To make the program a success, it's imperative you obtain their cooperation.

Therefore, your preliminary outline might look like this:

MESSAGE: Safety is the first priority of this company.

ACTION DESIRED BY THE AUDIENCE: Accept the changes and enthusiastically implement them on projects.

SAFETY SPEECH-OPENING

SAFETY SPEECH-BODY

A. The history of safety at our company has been the model for the industry.

1. Up to 18 months ago, we were listed in the top 10 companies in the region for safety.
2. On average, over the past 10 years, we've had only one serious injury per year.
3. We received awards from OSHA and other groups on our proactive approach to safety. (Show slide depicting the awards.)
   Segue: But over the last 18 months, everything has gone wrong!

B. The accidents over the last 18 months have injured our workers, members of our family, and our company's reputation. What went wrong?
   1. Summary of the accidents and injuries. (Show slide with the names of the injured employees.)
   2. While each accident may have separate causes, I'm more concerned with the culture of safety.
   3. We've become lax and complacent.
   4. Our safety training is outdated.
   5. As safety director, I assume responsibility for the failures, and that has to be shared with the project managers.
   Segue: We can't allow these failures to continue. We need to make changes immediately.

C. The culture of *Safety First* returns today, and the following changes require the support of us all.
   1. Training will be updated.

2. Random on-site safety inspections will take place.

3. Project managers and superintendents will be held accountable for safety on their job sites.

4. Safety bonuses will be initiated to provide additional incentive.

   Segue: Change cannot be accomplished by one person alone; all of us must make this a priority.

   (Show company president's statement on safety.)

SAFETY SPEECH-CLOSING

This simple preliminary outline admittedly requires work before it can be turned into a final product. However, it contains a clear message. The speaker knows what action the audience must take for this speech to be successful.

The outline follows the historical method: It lists the past history of safety success, turns to the current abysmal state analyzing what went wrong, then looks to the future and announces changes. Notice that a transition is included at the end of each section so the speech or presentation can move seamlessly from one point to another. The purpose of a transition is to provide a bridge between arguments. You may choose to employ other types of transitional techniques, such as asking a question that inevitably leads to the next point or using humor to phase in the next argument. Or you might want to construct transitional statements that incorporate the point just made as well as the point that follows.

The body of your speech is taking shape. Now you can take these written thoughts and turn them into a persuasive, dynamic speech.

CHAPTER 9

More on Writing the Speech

Speech is power: speech is to persuade,
to convert, to compel.
Ralph Waldo Emerson, American author
(1803-1882)

The words in your outline are written words that provide the structure of your speech. Your task becomes turning those thoughts into spoken language. To reiterate, you want to constantly build rapport with your audience, nudging your listeners ever closer to your position. This chapter includes a few techniques to help take the logic of your arguments and transform that logic into exciting, captivating language that moves your audience.

The Rule of Three

In our culture, statements grouped into segments of three capture the mind, so be sure to incorporate the use of triplets, or the rule of three, into your speeches or presentations when you can.

It's likely you know these famous triplets:

- life, liberty, and the pursuit of happiness (Thomas Jefferson)
- Veni, vidi, vici—I came, I saw, I conquered (Julius Caesar)
- government of the people, by the people, for the people (Abraham Lincoln)
- we cannot dedicate, we cannot consecrate, we cannot hallow this ground (Abraham Lincoln)

This rhetorical device, the rule of three, has been used for centuries as a means to trigger response from the audience, perhaps because of the proclivity of the human brain to remember items in groups of three. So in preparing a speech, it's a good idea to look for opportunities to group like concepts into a triplet formation. What worked for Thomas Jefferson, Julius Caesar, and Abraham Lincoln should work for you, too.

Figures of Speech

Other rhetorical devices known as figures of speech are also helpful. **Anaphora,** or the use of repetition for effect, can be one of the most dramatic of these devices.

With malice towards none;

With charity for all;

With firmness in the right. (Abraham Lincoln, Second Inaugural Address)

It was the best of times;

It was the worst of times;

It was the age of wisdom;

It was the age of foolishness. (Charles Dickens, *A Tale of Two Cities)*

I have a dream (repeated 8 times) (Martin Luther King, August 28, 1963)

A **simile** is a simple comparison using the words *like* or *as.* As President Ronald Reagan once said in a speech, "Education is like a diamond with many facets." Good similes evoke a response from the audience because they paint a simple but vivid picture of comparison.

Somewhat more complex is the **metaphor.** This figure of speech also creates a comparison, but in a more sophisticated way than the simile. Here's an example: "The Federal Reserve System is a giant heart pumping billions of dollars into the veins of our monetary system so they circulate through all the nation's banks." This metaphor compares the banking system to the human circulatory system. These devices aren't merely mental tricks; they're meant to help the audience understand.

Speakers use many other figures of speech to provide punch to their talks. The key? These devices create powerful pictures or associations that evoke an emotional spark. The logic of the argument follows, and the speaker gains rapport.

Storytelling

We like stories. We learn from stories. We are entertained by stories. They can make us laugh, cry, and even think. But not everyone is a storyteller.

Much like humor, storytelling requires pace and timing. Most important, whatever story you tell must support your argument. It may be historical or personal, but it must have a moral that furthers your cause. A good story helps build rapport; a bad story leaves everyone confused. If the story has meaning and supports your message, go with it. The story must be told with pace, which isn't as easy as it seems. You've likely heard someone tell a story or a joke that drones on and on. You want to jump in and scream, "Get on with it!"

To be effective, a story must have a certain quickness to it. It has to create drama. It must bewitch, not bore. If you think a story isn't just right for your purpose, then turn to another approach to deliver your argument or presentation.

Humor, Quotations, Numbers

To elucidate your points, you can use humor by telling a personal anecdote, for example. But, again, make sure the humor has a point and the point supports your arguments. Humor can be a great tool. As

President Reagan's speechwriter Peggy Noonan noted in her book *Simply Speaking*, "No one ever left a talk complaining that they laughed too often or too hard."[1] If you use quotations, you don't have to cite the work of origin exactly, but you do have to state who originally uttered the words.

Numbers and statistics can also be a good way to illustrate points, but remember that numbers can be twisted to suit any purpose. You always want your talk to represent the truth. So make the numbers you use clear, concise, and memorable. If you're using graphics for these points, make them exciting and easy to absorb.

The Words Themselves

Finally, let's consider the most important aspect of the speech—the words themselves. Your use of words is of paramount importance. If you can, stick to short Anglo-Saxon-based words. Long Latin-based words such as *facilitate* lack punch compared with *help*.

A few more examples of short powerful words

numerous	many
parameters	limits
expeditious	fast
utilize	use
methodologies	methods
enumerate	list

Some people believe that long words make them more authoritative. There is indeed a place for an extensive vocabulary *but not in a speech*. Having your audience understand your message quickly is your goal.

I suggest you read George Orwell's 1946 essay titled "Politics and the English Language." It should be mandatory reading for all speakers and authors. The author of the classic *1984* knew the power of language on the mind of men. In this essay, Orwell bemoans the state of the English language. He rails at the impreciseness of the writing, the wasted words. He then concludes that the author must choose the right word to fit the meaning—not to have the word dictate the meaning. He even set out six rules for clear writing, speaking, and thinking.

Here are Orwell's six rules:

1. Never use a metaphor, simile, or other figure of speech which you are used to seeing in print;
2. Never use a long word when a short one will do;
3. If it's possible to cut a word out, cut it out;
4. Never use the passive when you can use the active;
5. Never use a foreign phrase, scientific word, or a jargon word, if you can think of an everyday equivalent;
6. Break any of these rules sooner than say anything barbarous.

To further make his point, Orwell rewrote the famous Ecclesiastic quotation in modern English.

The original: *I returned and saw under the sun, that the race is not to the swift, nor the battle to the strong, neither yet bread to the wise, nor yet riches to men of understanding, nor yet favour to men of skill; but time and chance happeneth to them all.*

The sarcastically rewritten version by Orwell: *Objective considerations of contemporary phenomena compel the conclusion that success or failure in competitive activities exhibits no tendency to be commensurate with innate capacity, but that a considerable element of the unpredictable must invariably be taken into account.*

Jargon is more pronounced today than when Orwell wrote. So avoid it, steering clear of "corporate-speak" in your talks.

The list of corporate-speak phrases similar to these would fill another book, but as a start, stay away from:

- core competency,
- mission critical,
- tiger team,
- war room,
- let's circle back,
- all hands on deck,
- value-added,
- platform,
- and the most ridiculous one of all, open the kimono.

As Orwell said, speak in the active voice. In the active voice, the subject of the sentence does the action. At times, it's necessary to use passive-voice sentences, especially when you don't know *who* did the action. One example filling the airwaves today is "mistakes were made." It raises the question, "By whom?" Obviously, listeners aren't supposed to know. Using the active voice, though, the sentence would be "I made mistakes" or "people in my office made mistakes." The meaning becomes clearer immediately! So a dynamic presentation requires that you make your speech in the active voice whenever possible.

Don't hide your intent behind meaningless words such as *hopefully*, *probably*, or *possibly*. (Once, I forbade my staff from using any adverb other than *definitely* and it made a big difference.) Also watch out for phrases like "living quality" or "living document"—totally meaningless.

If you use a metaphor, make sure it's not one of the dying variety killed by overuse or the passage of time. For example, no one stands "shoulder to shoulder" anymore. Here are a few more expressions whose time has come and gone:

- axe to grind,
- ride roughshod over,
- toe the line.

If you talk in acronyms, quickly smack yourself in the face (figuratively, of course). While everyone may be familiar with RADAR (Radio Detection and Ranging), do we all know what OSHA is (Occupational Safety and Health Administration)? Or my personal favorite, COMCRUDESPAC (Commander Cruisers Destroyers Pacific)? It's YABA YABA YABA (Yet Another Bloody Acronym).

When you're speaking before professional or business groups, consider the jargon and acronyms of the industry. Not everyone knows that IPO stands for Initial Public Offering or that GSW means Gunshot Wound. If you're uncertain regarding the level of the group's understanding of certain terms, make sure you identify the meaning in a way that doesn't insult audience members. For example, "We're reviewing our IPO filing, which you probably know means our initial public offering filing." Better yet, get rid of the jargon and acronyms unless you're speaking to a group that clearly understands all of the terms you're using.

Rapport requires an initial emotional connection that you can accomplish with some of the techniques mentioned. But remember, intellectual backup must follow—and follow quickly. Ultimately, valid connection with those in your audience requires that your presentation stand both the test of logic and the test of truth.

Use all the tools in your rhetorical toolkit to make your speech spectacular and hook your audience—but also be logical, be clear, be sincere.

CHAPTER 10

The Audience,
Always the Audience

A speech is poetry: cadence, rhythm, imagery,
sweep! A speech reminds us that words, like
children, have the power to make dance the
dullest beanbag of a heart.
Peggy Noonan, American author and
speechwriter (1950-   )

You've crafted a dynamic opening. Your outline has taken shape, and your points are presented in a logical, orderly fashion. You're preparing dynamic slides to augment your arguments. All is going well—perhaps too well.

At some time during the preparation of your talk or presentation, a feeling of unease will overcome you. You'll wonder . . . "Will they get it? Will I move them? Will my plan work?"

If that feeling doesn't overcome you, then you're quite simply not doing your work at a deep enough level. It's normal for doubt to surface. When that happens, stop your preparation and think about the audience. *Always focus on the audience.*

Remember, all presentations, all speeches, all forms of communication are persuasive in nature. Even a talk designed to do nothing more than disseminate information is persuasive. You want your audience to accept the facts you're delivering. That's persuasion.

What do you know about the audience? All individuals are biased. Everyone sitting before you has preconceived intellectual and emotional notions. That's not bad; it's the nature of humans. Note that bias isn't prejudice, which means a predisposition based on ignorance or irrationality. Rather, bias is a predisposition based on personal preference and/or educational and social background.

When faced with a problem, people take an intellectual first step toward their personal bias. Sometimes an entire group is biased toward a position. For example, if I were speaking to a group of union delegates, I'd assume that the intellectual first step of the group would be pro-union with an anti-business bent. Likewise, if I were speaking to a group of business leaders on the question of union membership, I could reasonably assume a degree of anti-union bias.

Comparing a speaker's crafting of an exceptional speech with an artist's rendering of a masterpiece may lead us to conclude the speaker has a tougher road. After all, the artist's canvas is blank, giving the artist free rein. But the sea of people before a speaker is not blank. Individually and as a group, these people in the audience have various shades of intellectual color and depth. To a degree, they come before you "pre-painted." And with the advent of the Internet, the situation became even more complicated. With a mere click, we can find countless information. *But information isn't knowledge, and neither information nor knowledge equals wisdom.* To achieve knowledge, people apply critical thinking to information. Then wisdom results from testing knowledge through experience.

So why is your task as a public speaker more difficult today than in decades past? Because audience members *think they know.* They sit with personal biases, fully augmented with a flood of information in support of their intellectual first step. Your challenge is great because that intellectual first step may be *away from* your position.

So *your* first step is to return the thinking of audience members to a neutral position. Then you can work on persuading them to accept, or at the very least *consider*, that your argument holds merit and will benefit them or the organization's bottom line. Not an easy task.

With this in mind, find out everything you can beforehand about the emotional state of the audience. What's the age group? Its socioeconomic makeup? Are you speaking in the listeners' first language? Are you different from them? What do you have in common? Have they had any good or bad news lately? By chance, do you know anyone in the audience personally? Would it be appropriate to address that person directly in an attempt to build rapport—or would that embarrass the individual and be counterproductive?

Next, analyze the speaking event. Where is it being held? Who comes before you? After you? How many people are expected to attend? What does the audience expect?

Having reviewed your audience's needs, go back to your outline. You want to take the audience on your journey to the solution you offer, but you can be sure your listeners won't blindly follow you on this journey. A speaker once told me that in analyzing the audience and his attempt to persuade, he always assumed that audience members listened to WIIFM radio. Thus he had to answer their unstated question: What's In It For Me (WIIFM)? Only by acknowledging the need of the audience members to act in their own self-interest did he have a chance to persuade.

As you look at your outline again, you may want to present your talk as a problem/solution exercise, which is one of the more successful persuasive formats. Here's how it works:

1. Present the problem and show how it affects your audience.
2. Explain the problem with expertise.
3. Emphasize the depth of the difficulty.
4. Present your proposed solution.

5. If you sense the audience will question your solution, present several alternatives and show how and why they won't work.
6. Highlight the benefits of the solution you offer.
7. Make your listeners feel that what you offer is correct on both an emotional and an intellectual level.
8. Finally, get the audience to act, even in a small way, on something right then and there.

You want the motivation of your speech to last more than a few minutes after the presentation. As mentioned, one of the keys to a successful talk is to empower audience members to make a decision. A good persuasive speech leads listeners to one conclusion, which they accept because of the emotional and intellectual connection you've created. They make the solution their own because they decide based on the way you've led them to believe. *That* is the mark of a truly great speech.

How do you effectively close your speech? The next chapter provides ideas and guidance.

CHAPTER 11

Wrapping It Up—The Close

I do not object to people looking at their watches when I am speaking. But I strongly object when they start shaking them to make sure they are still going.
Lord Birkett, British jurist (1883-1962)

As it is with all good things, your talk must come to an end. Sometimes you'll just want to say "thank you" and sit down. But all great speeches or presentations have a closing, and you want your talks to be great. Besides, you've spent many an hour getting to this point, and you don't want to end your talk with a whimper.

The next section on presentation techniques reviews the advantages of writing out your entire speech. But no matter what technique you choose to prepare it, at the very least, write out the opening and the closing *word for word*. Your first and last impression should not be left to chance.

What do you want the closing to accomplish? In some way, you want to reiterate and emphasize the message. Perhaps you want listeners to take a particular action (e.g., wear safety gear), or maybe you want them to accept your argument and adopt it for themselves (e.g., support a certain candidate's ideas).

You can choose from several types of closings. In the summary closing, you reiterate the points you previously made and come full circle to your message. Personally, I stay away from this type of close. Once a speaker states, "Let me summarize," I notice an immediate rustling in the audience. People start packing up, realizing that the talk is over. They don't expect the speaker will be offering anything new.

Alternatively, you can close by reference—that is, referring to something that supports or is pertinent to your position. An inspirational closing may include a moving story or quotation to reinforce the emotional connection you hope you have made with the audience. And, yes, you can close with a laugh, using a humorous story that emphasizes the point of your speech.

My personal favorite involves a call to action. You'll have no greater measure of your success than when people in your audience act on the arguments you presented. For example, you might ask your listeners to spend, vote, change, engage, or accept—*but ask them to act*. If possible, get them to do a small thing right there in the room. For example, request a show of hands on a point or ask audience members to sign a petition. Indeed, if you presented your argument successfully, they'll be ready to act, to buy, to vote. As part of your closing, call for that action.

CHAPTER 12

Preparing for Delivery Day

They may forget what you said, but they will
never forget how you made them feel.
Carl W. Buechner, minister and author
(1926-)

When you stand in front of a group of people to talk—even for the shortest period of time—in some small way, you get *your* chance to change the world. Don't waste that chance. Spend time preparing your presentation.

At this point, you've completed the outline of your speech, and your opening and closing portions have been written out word for word.

Now you may find differing views on this next point. Some people believe you can advance your presentation by only following your outline. But in my opinion, that won't work. I say write it out. Don't take shortcuts. You simply can't tell if the speech is good or not unless you read it out loud. And you can't read it out loud if you don't write it.

Write your speech in a conversational style, just as you would talk to a friend. Rules of grammar don't apply for the first draft. Then once the speech is written out, use this draft to provide direction to yourself. As you reach a point where you want your voice to rise, then draw an arrow pointing up. Likewise, when you want your voice to fall, draw an arrow pointing down. If a pause is desired, insert the word PAUSE or draw a horizontal line indicating the break you want.

Because many words in the English language sound alike, make sure what you write is understandable. In *Simply Speaking,* Peggy Noonan points out that you may be talking about a saber, but the audience is hearing savior.[2] Underline in the text the points that have to be emphasized. As you read this first draft, you may find yourself out of breath. Perhaps the sentence is too long and requires a rewrite. At least insert a dash to tell yourself where to pause for a breath.

Not only must the words you choose be understandable, they must be easy to pronounce. Avoid words such as *ameliorate, obfuscate,* and *indomitable.* As fine as they are, they don't belong in a speech. So be direct and simple in your choice of language. As Ms. Noonan said: "Most of the important things that you will ever say or hear in life are composed of simple, good sturdy words. 'I love you,' 'It's over,' 'It's a boy,' 'He's dead.'"[3]

Writing out the speech also gives you the ability to spell names phonetically for proper pronunciation if need be. You're not afforded the luxury of mispronouncing anyone's name; that's a cardinal sin. But not everyone is named Smith or Jones, so take care on this point. In your speech, write out the name in a way that you can easily pronounce. For example, Mr. Gaitskhoki becomes Mr. GUYHOCKEY; Mr. Arshad becomes Mr. AH SHAD.

Remember, everyone (regardless of nationality or background) wants his or her name respected. I find that writing out names in this manner saves me a tremendous amount of embarrassment—and you will, too.

Once you've written out your speech, read it aloud—at least twice. Listen for any problems. Are the words clear and concise? Are you breathing properly throughout? Are you using voice inflection to emphasize the important points?

Think you're finished? Go back and revise the written words. Tighten up the language. Get rid of the qualifiers and other weasel words, such as "negative investment experience" and "impacting functionality." Check the directions you've given yourself. You may want to insert gestures or stage movements, such as "move toward the audience" or "lower voice—palms up." As you gain more experience before an audience, it shouldn't be necessary to insert these types of directions because they'll become natural to you. But if you're beginning, it may be helpful to plan your gestures and stage movements.

Unless you're speaking at the highest levels where every word is parsed and nuanced, you won't be reading your speech. Doing so runs counter to the goal of achieving rapport. Furthermore, it requires the use of a teleprompter. And reading the words from a screen while making it appear you're just conversing with the audience is among the highest of talents. Watch the television anchors on the major networks. To reach their level, they've mastered the technique of glancing at a portion of a sentence and quickly picking up the balance of the thought.

Reading your speech is out; so is memorizing it. If you do, you'll sound like a robot, and you can't easily react to the audience. Your goal is to reduce your written speech to several words that will help you flow from one segment to the next. How? The answer lies in the old joke: How do I get to Carnegie Hall? . . . Practice! Practice! Practice!

Practice your speech. Deliver your talk before a video camera (the camera doesn't lie). Give special attention to your transitions. Time your speech to make sure if fits within the requirements set forth. If possible, practice before a friend or loved one and try to ascertain the other person's reaction to your important points.

With each practice session, cut back on your notes until you reach the point where a mere word will trigger in your mind the entire segment of the speech. Chapter 8 described a speech by a corporate safety director talking about a sudden rise in field accidents on various construction sites. With practice, he can reduce his notes to prompt words such as THE PAST. His mind should be able to go to the portion of the speech where he sets forth the exemplary safety record of the company. Then he can use as the next prompt words WHAT HAPPENED. That should trigger the portion of the speech that explains the sudden rise in accidents.

To use prompt words well, be confident in your speech. That requires rehearsing it *so often* that the content becomes part of you.

If this entire routine seems like a great deal of work, guess what—it is! When you accept the challenge of speaking before a group, you accept a moral responsibility of a sort. Let me share a warning. As the number of your speaking engagements increases, your proficiency will grow and these steps will come easier to you. The time will come when you'll be tempted to eliminate a step or two. Beware! Remember the words of the famed pianist Franz Liszt (1811-1886):

If I miss one day's practice, I notice it;
If I miss two days' practice, the critics notice it;
If I miss three days' practice, the public notices it.

With that, keep in mind that if you short-circuit the routine of adequate in-depth practice, you'll find that someday one of your talks will fall flat. When you analyze what went wrong, your mind will know you cheated on the preparation. There are no shortcuts.

Here's another dose of reality: No speech will be delivered exactly as you prepared it. As Dale Carnegie once said: "There are always three speeches for every one you actually gave. The one you practiced, the one you gave, and the one you wish you gave."

You'll always leave the speech realizing it was delivered differently than you prepared to give it. Perhaps you left something out. Or you put something in. Or you didn't say something the way you wanted to. Every speaker has the same feeling and realization. It's simply a learning process.

Remember your purpose—to achieve rapport with the audience, speak in a conversational tone, and persuade the audience in some fashion. If you accomplished all that, don't sweat the small stuff. There is no perfect speech. Remember, Lincoln didn't like his famous Gettysburg address when he sat down.

It takes time and effort to give even a 20-minute talk. No one can "wing it." This is your chance to effect change; make the best of it!

CHAPTER 13

More Preparations for Performance

There are two things that are more difficult
than making an after-dinner speech: climbing
a wall which is leaning toward you and
kissing a girl who is leaning away from you.
Winston Churchill,
British politician and author (1874-1965)

You've practiced your speech until everyone in your house or office avoids you. You've reduced the written speech to a few trigger words and completely memorized the opening and closing. You've spent time working on the transitions from one argument to another, and you're convinced the message is clear and the audience will understand.

Nervous Habits

As you get close to finishing your preparation, consider that you *will* be nervous. That's the nature of public speaking. But don't let the fears and nervousness hold you back. If you've followed the guidelines in previous chapters, you'll be prepared.

That said, watch out for how that nervousness might affect your presentation. Nervous habits such as playing with your notes, running your hands through your hair, and touching parts of your face can be quite distracting. Ironically, despite your hours of practice, these nervous "ticks" don't surface until you're in front of a live audience, even if you practiced your talk before a video camera.

Once I was conducting a daylong seminar before 125 people. From the audience's reaction, the laughter, and the participation level, I thought the event was going well. During the first break, a member of the audience came up to me to say it was going well but I should stop jiggling the change in my pocket. I didn't even *know* I was doing it. I had allowed my natural nervousness to trickle down my arm and dissipate from my fingers to my change. Unfortunately, people could hear the jingling and it distracted them. On occasion, I still put my right hand in my pants pocket, but my change and keys remain safely in my coat jacket.

Have someone watch your presentation, or if it's recorded, review it. Watch for signs of nervousness that you can correct in your next talk.

Also watch for filler words, sounds, or expressions such as *Er . . . Uh . . . Well . . . Y' know*. These words signal uncertainty. They happen when the mind isn't in sync with the mouth, i.e., we're talking faster than we're thinking—or conversely, we've forgotten what comes next and need filler while we remember. Not only are these fillers distracting, they are hallmarks of an unprofessional speaker.

I vividly recall listening to a speech by the president of a company at a corporate event. My partner at the table and I were keeping track of the number of "ahs" he said, and we completely lost his message. Once again, a nervous habit likely won't surface during your preparation. So what can you do? Have someone look for this type of distraction, report them to you, and then rid your talk of such useless mutterings. Slow down your speech. Give your brain a chance to catch up to your mouth.

Ironically, President Reagan's trademark was to start most of his impromptu sentences with the word *well*. In fact, his use of *well* rose to comic proportions. It worked for him, but you aren't an accomplished actor—nor are you president of the United States. You'd best avoid anything that will distract the audience from absorbing your message.

Gestures

The age of fiery oratory is over. No longer do we see a William Jennings Bryant standing on stage with his head bent forward, hands raised to the sky mimicking a crucifixion, and closing with "You shall not crucify mankind upon a cross of gold!" The age of television has invited amazing speakers into the confines of our home and created personal experiences. Look at the network television anchors. The movement of their hands is imperceptible; their expressions are smoothly conveyed in their faces.

Nevertheless, when speaking to a live audience, gestures are important—but they must be natural and mirror the spoken word. The problem of unnatural gestures existed even in Shakespeare's day. As Hamlet instructed the actors:

> "Nor do not saw the air too much with your hand thus, but use all gently . . . Suit the action to the word, the word to the action."[4]

Members of your audience will know immediately if your gestures are unnatural. Yes, you can punch the air if you wish to make a point. After all, you're trying to garner rapport with the audience. Open up your arms, palms up, to create an appearance of openness. But always be natural and in complete sync with the spoken word.

That leads to the often-asked question, "What do I do with my hands?" My answer is always the same: What do you *normally* do with your hands when you speak to someone? Do you keep one hand in your pocket when you talk and gesture with the other hand? That's fine. Putting both hands in your pockets won't work, and of course, women often don't have pockets to worry about. I suggest keeping your hands at your sides if you're comfortable doing so. Just be aware of and avoid nervous habits such as combing your hands through your hair or touching your face.

Most important, try not to think about *yourself*. Think about the audience. Focus always on what is needed to bring them closer to you and your position. I've said it before and I'll say it again; that's the measure of a successful speech or presentation.

Voice

The most powerful tool we have in public speaking is the voice. A successful speaking voice must have presence and resonance. Presence is the quality of a voice that permits it to stand out and be heard, while resonance is the quality that makes the voice sound rich and pleasant. Presence comes from permitting the voice to leave the throat and enter the facial area, touching the facial cavities. Resonance results from speaking at the proper pitch and not forcing or straining the voice.

If you feel your voice doesn't convey presence or resonance, do breathing exercises or hum a few bars of a song. Then you'll feel the sound moving around in your nasal cavities. Breathe deeply and expand your stomach, letting the air leave from the diaphragm. With practice, your voice will fill a room.

Varying the tone and speed of your speech creates pace. You can race with your voice up to the precipice of a cliff and then stop, pause, and slow down as you make an important point. Pace—that is, changes in tone, pitch, volume, and speed—makes your voice more interesting. When asking a question, the voice should naturally rise at the end of the question. But when making statements, your sentence should start normally, rise as the important point is reached, and then return to normal at the end of the statement.

Work on these tips. They're getting you closer to speaking day.

CHAPTER 14

The Tools of the Trade

There is no power like that of true oratory.
Caesar controlled men by exciting their fears;
Cicero by captivating their affections and
swaying their passions. The influence of one
perished with its author; that of the other
continues to this day.
Henry Clay, congressman (1777-1852)

Gone are the days when you could just stand before a group and make an exceptional presentation without the use of audiovisual equipment. Before you utter one word, you have to know certain facts about the event:

- How many people will be in attendance?
- What type of room will be used?
- How will the seating be arranged?
- Does the forum provide the equipment, or is that the speaker's responsibility?
- Is an HDTV big screen available in the room?

Once you have the answers to these questions, then analyze the equipment you'll need.

Microphone

Let's look at a few mainstays. Of course, if you're speaking or making a presentation to a small group, your natural speaking voice should fill the room. If the space is large, however, or if more than 20 people are in attendance, be sure to augment your voice with a microphone. Many models and types are available. Years ago, the use of microphones was limited by the length of the cable that connected the device to the transmitter. Those days are history. You can now choose to use a lavaliere microphone—a wireless device you can hook up to your lapel or shirt. Its transmitter can be mounted on your body or a nearby table.

Another option is a head-mounted microphone. This type involves a lightweight headset that goes over your ear then juts out beside your face, with the end piece near your mouth. The advantage, of course, is that this model provides full freedom for your hands. In the past, these types of headsets were generally large and black. Today, the headset is clear, almost imperceptible, and omni-directional. In other words, the microphone solves the problem of your voice dropping off when you turn your head.

My personal favorite is the handheld wireless microphone. Using this mic helps with my natural nervousness by giving me something to hold. It's also a good tool for interaction with the audience. If your program dictates that you move around among the participants, you can hand someone the microphone for a question or comment that can be heard by the entire audience. Unless you're experienced in using the handheld device, however, you'll be subject to voice drop-off. When you turn your head or change direction from one part of the audience to another, make sure the mic follows. Hold it close enough to your mouth to permit amplification.

Remember, the sound amplification is a complete system requiring the microphone, transmitter, and speakers. Many venues maintain their own audiovisual departments and specialists. These individuals are professionals, and their expertise is vital to setting up your room for an effective presentation. If such service isn't available, then it's your responsibility to obtain what you need.

Visuals

You will almost certainly want some type of visual to accompany your speech or presentation. In the recent past, visual presentations have been projected from a laptop onto a screen or sometimes a television with a wireless setup. The use of a laptop for that purpose marked a substantial technological advancement. Gone were slide projectors for photographs and overhead projectors with cumbersome transparencies, which used to be the main tools of public speakers.

Although presenters still use laptops, even that tool is becoming passé. PowerPoint presentations can be placed on tablets, handheld devices, and even smart phones. If the venue has HDTV available, wireless hookups can be used to transmit the presentation to the TV. In venues that don't have TV access, a mobile device can be connected to a projector. When a laptop is used, the presenter triggers slide changes with a remote device. On a tablet or smart phone, especially if there's a wireless connection, a mere swipe of the screen will have the same effect. The use of audiovisual in a presentation is an industry all to itself. Bill Johnson's website (www.speakerstools.com) provides insightful information on various devices available.

But be forewarned: Become proficient in whatever system you use and make sure everything works. Remember that the more complicated the system, the more likely Murphy's Law will rear its ugly head; i.e., anything that can go wrong, will go wrong. Always be prepared for something to go wrong. If your speech or presentation was properly prepared, the visual devices augment your message but aren't a mainstay. Consider them dispensable so you can return to your points and pound away at your message without them if necessary.

At last, after all of the work, preparation, and practice, the day of your presentation has finally arrived. Now what?

CHAPTER 15

Speech Delivery Day!

Is sloppiness in speech caused by ignorance or apathy? I don't know and I don't care!
William Safire, American author and speechwriter (1929-2009)

Have you followed the instructions in the previous chapters? Good! You're prepared. You can deliver your talk or presentation with confidence.

Let's say you intend to talk for 20 or 30 minutes. Looking back, it's hard to believe the hours of work required to get you to this point. At this point, all of your efforts and preparation must coalesce into a dynamic, persuasive talk. But even before one word leaves your lips, you still have more to do.

Be sure to get to the site of your presentation early. The last thing you want to feel is panic caused by rushing around to get everything done at the last minute. Check out the room to make sure the lighting is proper and the seating arrangements are as planned. Will the seats be classroom style with tables or auditorium style with chairs only? Walk around the room. If you plan to move around during the presentation, do so during your walkthrough. Break the room down into quadrants.

Remember, eye contact is imperative, so during this walkthrough, let your eyes pick focus locations based upon the quadrants you've identified.

Set up your equipment. Get with the IT or audiovisual people to make sure everything works. Check everything more than once. Run through your PowerPoint presentation and make sure the slides are in proper order. No one wants to sit there during the presentation waiting for the PowerPoint to load. *You have to be ready to go.*

Smile when your audience arrives. If it's a small group, introduce yourself to those who arrive first. If it's a large group and a moderator will be introducing you, talk with that person and make sure your introduction is complete. Ascertain whether any last-minute changes need to be made in the program.

Finally, it's time. The introduction is over, and your name is called. You grab the microphone, take the stage, and gaze at the audience. What you've spent hours preparing and practicing must now flow out of you with ease and brilliance.

It will.

CHAPTER 16

Video Conferences, Webcasts, and Other Technological Complications

Be nice to nerds.
Chances are you'll end up working for one.
Bill Gates, American business magnate (1955-   )

From the time humans first harnessed the power of fire and invented the wheel, we sought tools to assist us in achieving our goals. Today, practically every desk in every business has a computer. Nearly every backpack we see on the street contains a computer tablet. Smart phones are proliferating, providing instantaneous communication around the world. If we watch a movie from the late 1990s or early 2000s, we giggle when we see the large bulky monitors. These screens that seemed such an advancement at the time have been relegated to museum status by the thin, sleek screen devices we own.

Of course, the world of public speaking is also constantly evolving because technology advances daily. Today, we have videoconferencing in which seminars and speeches can connect participants from around the globe. People can subscribe to podcast and video series that download at regular intervals to their computer or portable device for listening and viewing. Web conferencing enables items on a participant's computer to be shared with other conferees if need be. We can convene simply by clicking a mouse or touching a tablet screen. And yet, despite all the advancements in technology, people appear to be growing further apart.

Some wise person once said, "The more things change, the more they stay the same." In the realm of public speaking, there's no greater truth. For despite the advances in communication inherent in the use of the computer and the Internet, the underlying reality stays the same—that all communication seeks to persuade someone. That persuasion may take the form of motivation to act on something or education to ensure as much as possible that the audience understands and agrees with the information provided. *This reality never changes*.

Ironically, all of the technological advancements place a *greater* burden on the speaker to ensure people in the audience understand the message and yield to the arguments.

My main premise is that successful public speaking depends on achieving a level of rapport with the audience. But achieving this unity is difficult. It takes hard work. Anyone who's stepped in front of an audience or made a sales presentation will attest to this fact. But at least before the onslaught of computer advancements, you had listeners right there with you. You could see their faces, look into their eyes, and gauge their bodily responses to your arguments. You could make them part of the presentation.

Today, an audience member is a face on a screen, if that, and participants can be scattered all over the globe. The problem being addressed—how to achieve rapport—is magnified with every computer or TV screen.

There are webinars where participants can type in a question or comment, and teleseminars where participants can electronically raise their hands by pressing a button on a phone. Despite having the intent of bring the speaker closer to the audience, these tools still make true rapport difficult to achieve.

The desire to see the person you're talking to is not new. The Bell Telephone pavilion in the 1964 New York World's Fair touted Picture Phones. The picture was black and white, but you could speak to another party and clearly see them talk back to you. Although the promise of videoconferencing hasn't, of yet, been fully achieved, technology will continue to advance. Before long, even the smallest business will have the network necessary to quickly access and participate in presentations from the other side of the globe.

One reason videoconferencing hasn't fully arrived is that, despite the advances in technology, concerns remain. Videoconferencing isn't easy. Problems inherent in transmissions may require troubleshooting and hence create delay. In addition, conferencing equipment is still expensive and must be coordinated with each participant's system.

More interesting, perhaps, is that people seem to resist its use. They feel more stilted talking on screen. Subconsciously, they're uncertain who may be viewing them. Anxiety is increased not only in the participants but also in the facilitator or speaker. It also appears that participants have to work harder to interpret the information provided in video conferences.

As younger generations enter the workplace with their social networking skills, the use of videoconferencing will increase as the stated concerns dissipate. Of course, the technology will become easier to use, too. Widespread availability of videoconferencing will in time become a reality.

Herein, the speaker faces a conundrum. Building rapport is necessary to successfully communicate, yet the video conference or the computer screen places another barrier to achieving some degree of unity with the audience. For a speaker or facilitator, just a few of the challenges to be addressed include identifying who is talking, detecting movement, securing eye contact, and taking turns among the participants.

Suffice it to say, you'll have to work harder to conduct a successful video conference than an in-person face-to-face talk. You'll need to:

- send the agenda and copies of any slides to remote locations well in advance of the conference.
- work out the protocols with all of the locations to determine speaking order and how participation will be controlled.
- make sure participants know how to use their mute button to ensure that any talking at the remote location won't be carried over the network.

On a technical note, as the speaker you'll have enough to do, so have someone else operate any cameras. Eye contact is a problem because people tend to look into the screen, but to look into the other person's eyes, you have to look at the camera. In fact, this constitutes yet another issue that's held back the use of videoconferencing. Early in 2012, however, new software using 3D imaging has evolved that solves the problem. Using this software will permit you to look straight into the screen and see the other person looking back. Commercialization of this software is expected by the end of 2013.

Building rapport depends on feedback from the audience. You, as the speaker or facilitator, must constantly monitor understanding from the remote locations, obtaining feedback more often than a face-to-face conference. Frequent questioning of the remote locations to ascertain comprehension is a must. Not only that, but it's important to obtain feedback in quick bursts or you'll risk losing the attention of the other remote locations.

In short, the challenges of driving home your point in a persuasive fashion are greater in the computer age. However, you can't afford to sacrifice rapport when using audio and video tools. Take care to provide an audience-centered experience, even if that audience is miles or even continents away.

CHAPTER 17

The Dreaded Meeting

*Meetings are indispensable when you don't
want to do anything.*
John Kenneth Galbraith,
American economist (1908-2008)

At any given moment of the business day in the United States, 25 million people are involved in meetings. No doubt you'll partake in a least one of these business gatherings before the end of your business week.

Meetings are a paradox. On one hand, they're an essential part of the communication process in an organization. People are supposed to solve problems in these group sessions and share information between the various business divisions or other entities. And yet, despite their vital nature, meetings can be frustrating. Few participants enjoy them because they tend to be routine, boring, and unproductive. Often no one acts on the decisions attendees supposedly made, and matters are left hanging for the next meeting.

You may never be called on to captivate an audience numbering in the hundreds, and you may never have to make a dynamic presentation to a group. But you will no doubt be called upon to either lead a meeting or present your views at one of them. You didn't enter the business world to be a wallflower. While the forum may be different from that of standard speeches, the same concepts of rapport and persuasion apply to the meeting room. Speaking at meetings will probably be your first experience in addressing an audience in the business arena, and understanding the dynamics of a successful meeting are essential to your advancement. Thus, let's address this essential forum in more detail.

Why all the pain and dissatisfaction around meetings? Simply stated, the average meeting fails to function as it should. Your first question should always be: Is a meeting necessary in the first place?

Meetings take place for the following reasons.

- **To disseminate information.** The group's leader has vital information that must be shared with the staff to ensure a smooth flow for the project. Perhaps the purpose is to announce a decision that affects everyone there. In this age of email, the leader should look carefully at the need to call a meeting. Surely less costly means exist to transmit information to all who need it. The leader is advised to call the meeting only if it's necessary to ensure that everyone understands the information. Sometimes a leader must deliver it in person to answer questions, check reactions, and make certain the facts have sunk in, as well as ensure proper implementation.

- **To receive information.** Often the most important reason for a meeting is to receive information. The leader of the group needs to receive periodic updates from staff on the progress of various projects. In this instance, information flows in the opposite direction, from the staff to the leader. Be careful, however, when it comes to problems. While a good leader needs and wants to know about problems, many people don't want to address them in front of their colleagues. Office politics, egos, and futures are involved. A good leader fosters an atmosphere in which people can talk in private if they wish to—without the risk of embarrassment or public recrimination.
- **To solve problems.** No one person has all the answers. The meeting is a perfect device to raise problems and pool the thoughts and ideas of the staff to find solutions.
- **To put on a "dog and pony" show.** The big production. These types of meetings are often conducted so many individuals can present some form of a show. Businesses use these productions to, for example, announce a new product. In these types of meetings, the meeting leader assumes the role of a presenter, and all the rules of preparation apply.

The bottom line: Some meetings are necessary, so you'll have to deal with this reality. As a leader, you can learn how to run more dynamic, effective sessions. But first you must always ask: Is a meeting necessary in this situation? If so, how long should it last?

When planning a meeting, keep in mind the following points.

Meetings mean money ($). Everyone sitting at that table is paid to be there. True, some more than others, but everyone attending has some rate of pay. Often leaders examine the cost of the smallest detail of any project to the third decimal place but fail to place a monetary value on the endless hours spent in meetings. Every minute spent in non-productive activity around a meeting table delays other work that must be accomplished. Even in this computerized age, people still can't effectively complete two tasks at the same time, and meetings occupy a substantial portion of the work schedule.

No meeting should start without attendees knowing when it's going to end! The first words out of the mouth of the meeting leader should always state the length of the meeting, even if it was announced via email beforehand. Something such as, "People, let's wrap up within an hour" would suffice. Or perhaps, "Let's resolve this installation problem before lunch." Setting a time limit is vital. Talk seems to expand to fill the time allotted, and if none is specified, participants can ramble for hours. For some strange reason, people tend to work more efficiently with a deadline. The role of the leader is to evaluate the reason for the meeting and establish a fair timeframe that will resolve the purpose of the session. Today, Outlook and other email notification systems normally include the ending time in a meeting invitation, which is a step in the right direction. The leader must then reinforce the deadline at the opening of the meeting.

Only necessary participants should attend. Entourages should be left to the sports superstar. The leader needs to invite only the people vital for the purpose of the meeting. If the meeting is to disseminate company-wide information, for example, the heads of groups can attend, then pass along the news to their individual charges as they deem appropriate. The magic number for conducting business is *five*. If fewer than five people attend, the leader risks not having an adequate sampling of opinion. If more than five attend, the meetings tend to wander because each person seeks to place a personal agenda on the table.

One meeting should have one purpose. If possible, the meeting leader should limit the purpose of the meeting to a single goal. If you are the leader and wish to provide information, give it and then adjourn. If the purpose of the meeting is to solve a problem, solve it and then adjourn. Avoid giving information and then delving into a problem. Having multiple purposes tends to extend the length of the meeting, create wandering, and lose interest and possibly attendees. If the meeting must have more than one purpose, then address the purpose that affects the most attendees first. Once that function is over, the non-essential participants can leave, allowing the rest to address the remaining concerns.

Sometimes the answer is more meetings, not fewer. This may come as a surprise, but more meetings may be required. At a normal meeting, occasionally participants raise problems that no one thought of before. Rather than spend the entire group's time addressing this new concern, the leader can recognize the importance of the problem and immediately establish a sub-group to explore it. This smaller group can devise solutions and report back to the main meeting group within a specified period. This permits the main meeting to stay on track while setting in motion a mechanism to resolve the problem. More and smaller meetings can thus sometimes be more effective than dragging out larger meetings.

Is an agenda necessary? Every meeting requires an agenda, right? Not necessarily. At times, it appears a pre-meeting meeting is necessary merely to establish the agenda. Agenda outlines can be extremely formal, listing in detail every facet of concern. Others may provide only general ideas to be addressed. Both can be productive. Some of the most effective meetings, however, have no agenda. The leader goes around the table giving each attendee one minute to express any burning questions he or she may have. No discussion takes place until all the attendees have had their minute.

The items put forward then become the agenda for the meeting.

If you're the leader, use your public speaking skills. The meeting is a forum, thus a flow of participation is required for it to be effective. As leader of the meeting, seek to establish rapport with the group. Be sure to use some of the same devices previously discussed for giving a speech. Here, however, you'll have more participation. Control the conversation so participants don't wander off target, and ask questions to bring the participants back to the point. Use eye contact to determine if the group is "getting" it. No rule says that all members of the meeting have to sit around a table. You don't want everyone to become too comfortable. Stand up if you need to establish rapport. In fact, I recall a time when I removed the chairs and we all stood. Otherwise, meetings tended to drone on and on. It was a blessedly short meeting—and extremely productive.

Summarize and follow up. Just as you prepared your speech with a structure (opening, body, and closing), meetings can follow a similar pattern. Your opening is important because it announces to all what you hope to accomplish. The body of the meeting is the discussion that takes place: the questions asked, the problems raised and resolved. When you close a meeting, it's imperative to summarize the actions decided, who is responsible for follow-up in what areas, and how much time they have for completion. And finally, record the results somewhere. If your industry requires formal minutes, than prepare them quickly. If a summary email will suffice, that's fine. But get it out to the participants before you forget.

To run an effective, dynamic meeting, remember one word as your guide: *alacrity*. Alacrity refers to an enthusiastic quickness. That's the secret of an effective meeting. Run the group with passion and enthusiasm, add a large dose of quickness, and the recipe is complete.

CHAPTER 18

Modern Business Etiquette

If you're not 15 minutes early; you are late!
Vince Lombardi, American football coach
(1913-1970)

Throughout this book, I've stressed the vital importance of rapport. Whether you're conducting a presentation, a small seminar, or a speech before a packed auditorium, your success depends on establishing a relationship with your audience.

The essence of a successful relationship—for whatever purpose—lies in civility. Certainly, our dealings today lack the strict formality that once existed in society. Nevertheless, simple etiquette demonstrating courtesy and caring is essential.

Let's consider a few examples of bad manners commonly seen today. I'm sure you can expand the list to include your own pet peeves.

The Problem of Lateness

Personally, I detest lateness. All speeches, presentations, seminars, and meetings have a start time.

In my experience, it's impossible to count the number of important business functions delayed or disrupted by a participant arriving 15 minutes or more after the start time. The person enters, often with papers under arm and a wave of the hand as if to ask forgiveness for being late. Lateness tells me the person is selfish. Is that individual's time more important than anyone else's in the room? Lateness also tells me the person is rude and uncaring. Who wants to make that impression? I trust not you.

Famed football coach Vince Lombardi had a 15-minute rule requiring all players to be in attendance and *in place* 15 minutes early, whether it was for a team meeting or class. He believed that such a requirement showed discipline and respect to all involved. Today, the clock at Lambeau Field, the home of the Green Bay Packers, is set 15 minutes early in honor of the Lombardi rule. I wouldn't argue with the recipes for success imposed by this winner of four NFL championships and the first two Super Bowls.

Incidentally, one of Lombardi's disciples, Tom Coughlin, is head coach of the New York Giants. He gave his players more leeway and cut the time requirement from 15 to only five minutes. But even the requirement of arriving five minutes early for various activities caused angst among the players. Several rebelled and the team imposed numerous fines. Two Super Bowl wins later, no one in the New York Giants' organization argues about arriving early for meetings.

Be on time. Be prepared.

True, life happens and, on occasion, you will be justifiably late. If so, always call. Civility demands you respect others and their time. Courtesy mandates calling the first moment you suspect you may be late. (By the way, people intuitively know if you're late because of a flat tire or because you couldn't get out of bed, given your activities the night before.)

Electronics and the Loss of Common Courtesy

People today have smart phones, tablets, and even nearly extinct laptops. These devices create a different set of civility concerns. Part of the problem, I believe, is the way we humans are internally wired. We can be having a face-to-face conversation with an individual, important or otherwise, when suddenly we sense a vibration or hear an inane tone emanating from our pocket or bag. Instantaneously, without any thought, our eyes drift down. The attention we were giving the other person immediately dissipates. What makes that instant message we received—that newly arrived email causing the vibration in our pocket or even the phone call—more important than the human being standing in front of us? It's plain rude.

Once we've viewed the message or email, our concentration with the conversation is broken, and we must pick up where we left off. What should have taken a minute or two is now extended by the counterproductive interruptions. We simply can't split our focus and concentration between two competing forces.

In truth, we're all interconnected with a myriad of devices. But good decision-making and proper action require focus. In the meeting room, the seminar, the presentation, and the speech, those interruptions that didn't even exist 15 years ago create an additional impediment to achieving rapport.

When I'm conducting a seminar and I see laptops out or smart phones on the table, I always wonder what percentage of the participants are taking notes and what percentage are checking emails or the nightly scores on ESPN.

How to Deal with Electronic Interruptions

As if obtaining rapport weren't difficult enough, today's speaker must work even harder to achieve success. As a leader, you need to establish rules. At the outset, you can ask that phones be turned off or at least put on vibrate so they won't disrupt the session. Ideally, you want the audience to turn off their devices. What you're talking about is important to them or they wouldn't be there, so it's in their best interests to concentrate on the message you're sending their way. In most instances, that ideal is wishful thinking.

Here, you might actually attempt to negotiate with your audience. Let them know you acknowledge they're busy and have other important interactions going on. Ask them to turn their devices off, and then tell them you'll schedule frequent email breaks during the session. That way, their needs can be satisfied.

Also recognize that emergencies do exist and say that, if the rare occasion should arise that a call or email must be answered immediately, you request it be taken outside the room. Encourage the audience to agree with you that the vast majority of messages can wait for a while. Tell them that, for a few minutes, you intend to free them from this burden of having to reply to their avalanche of emails. Get them working *with* you. Seeing fingers wailing away in response to an inane email message is rude not only to the speaker but to the other participants in the room.

The reality of these interruptions makes your opening all the more important. If your presentation is powerful and riveting, the audience will gladly, for a time, accept your offer to free them from the humdrum burdens housed in the vast majority of electronic devices.

CHAPTER 19

Are There Any Questions?

If there are no stupid questions, then what
kind of questions do stupid people ask?
Do they get smart just in time to ask
questions?
Scott Adams, American cartoonist (1955-   )

Having questions at the end of your presentation create a paradox. On one hand, nothing excites speakers more than receiving questions because they can then ascertain if the audience received their message. Did the listeners "get" it? Questions also help determine if the speaker achieved rapport, so seeing numerous hands up when questions are solicited at the end of the presentation should be welcomed.

Paradoxically, questions asked by audience members offer an opportunity for people to press opposing agendas or cite opposite points of view. Sometimes these questions are extremely critical and can sidetrack or even hijack the speaker's entire message.

The worst scenario? The speaker calls for questions only to hear a tittering in the crowd and see no hands up. The speaker then says, "No questions? Well, thank you" and slinks off to the side to a modicum of applause. This is one of the main differences between a speech and a presentation. If you're making a formal speech before a group, questions may not be part of the agenda. But during presentations, especially in the business realm, speakers seek out questions from the audience. While it is indeed possible that your talk so convinces everyone that questions are unnecessary, that's rarely the case.

After your talk, if you receive no questions from the audience, it can mean only a few things:

- Your speech was too long.
- You violated a sensitivity in the crowd, such as an inadvertent cultural remark. This is easy to do and, if it goes unrecognized by the speaker, will not be forgiven by the audience.
- The audience dismissed your position quickly.
- You didn't "reach" your listeners in a meaningful way, or the speech was so convoluted, they grew tired of trying to follow your logic.

Receiving no questions at the end of your talk is generally a mark of failure. However, if you've followed the dictates of this book, I'm certain that won't be the response from *your* audience.

Handling Questions

Successful public speaking mandates mastering the art of handling questions. These exchanges are an opportunity to increase your rapport with the audience *and* reinforce the points you made in your talk. That said, this opportunity is fraught with peril, so here are a few pointers:

The speech isn't over when you think it is. Be prepared for the questions and don't relax once you've concluded your talk. Anticipate what the group might ask.

Don't answer a question too quickly. Take a few seconds to think about it. This creates the impression that the question is valid and you're giving it the time it deserves. The pause shows you're a pensive person.

Tell the truth. If you try to dodge the truth, the audience will catch you and it will jeopardize your entire position. If you don't know an answer, say so!

Learn how to turn, or bridge, the question. This tactic is the staple of politicians, but it's useful in numerous situations as well. It permits the speaker to give credence to the question and, by inference, to the person asking the question. But then the speaker turns, or bridges, the argument to reinforce the position of the message just given. *Note:* People may see this tactic as evasive, so use it sparingly.

Here are a few examples of turning, or bridging, the question:

"I don't think anyone can give a realistic answer to that question, but I *can* say . . ."

"Sure that's important, but have you thought about . . . ?"

"I don't know the answer to that, but isn't the most important question . . . ?"

Make sure that what's being asked is really a question. Many times, the person asking is actually making a suggestion, and there's a substantial difference between the two. As a speaker, you have to recognize when someone is, in fact, presenting a different idea. Sometimes these questions can be hostile. They may start as, "I understand your point, but what about . . . ?" Then the questioner starts off in another direction. If what is suggested is a good idea, say so. If it's a lousy idea (and we've all had ideas of this type), be careful not to embarrass the questioner. You can put discussing the idea on hold until after the meeting to get it off the table.

Beware of questioners who are crusading for their own agenda. These people are using this forum to press a point that's important to them. It may not even involve the subject of your talk. And with only one question, the group can be taken far afield in seconds. Always control the room, but you have to do so in a manner that's perceived as fair so you won't lose your rapport with the rest of the group. You might say something like this (assuming it's true): "I don't have the authority to resolve your issue, but there's someone in my company who does. I'll contact that person today and forward you a copy of my email explaining your concern. Let me finish and I'll do what I can—but I need the next twenty minutes to cover what I was asked to present."

Keep the question-and-answer period short. The longer the time you allocate to this part of the presentation, the greater the likelihood your message will become diluted. End the session with participants' hands still in the air if necessary. Use the last question you take as a means to reinforce the essence of your message. This should be treated as a secondary close. You want to leave the group with your message in their mind, so keep control of your final close.

Remember that most questioners aren't asking questions, they're seeking approval. In time, with practice, you can use the information requested by the questioner in a fashion that shows the person respect and approval while still reinforcing your own message.

CONCLUSION

Dare to Speak!!

*There are three things to aim at in public
speaking: first, to get into your subject;
then to get the subject into yourself;
and lastly, to get the subject into the heart of
your audience.*
Alexander Gregg,
first Episcopalian bishop of Texas
(1819-1893)

What you think is important! What you say is important! Quite simply, *you* are important!

But no one will know unless you muster the courage to face the crowd. Your audience may number in the hundreds or it may consist of a few members of your business group exploring solutions to a problem. Dare to speak! Follow the rules and techniques outlined in this book, and with practice, you'll be able to grasp the power to persuade, convert, compel, and get your message into the hearts and minds of people in your audience.

The game plan in preparing to speak is quite simple. Let's review the concepts.

You, as the speaker, must find a way to become one with the audience, to achieve the heralded state of rapport. To do this, you can apply a few constants.

First, rapport depends on achieving emotional connection with the audience. This connection must be subtle, or you could be accused of being manipulative. (More on manipulation follows.) Rather, the aim is to achieve a slight emotional tug on the audience.

Once you make that connection, the logic of your message should be forceful, impeccable, and in the best interests of the audience. True persuasion requires both an emotional connection and a logical message.

Finally, be sure to end with a call to action.

Persuasion versus Manipulation

Throughout, this book has stated that the end of all forms of communication is persuasion. The form may be a simple smile or a "good morning" that seeks a pleasant response and an emotional bond in return. Or it may be a major presentation, pitching millions of dollars' worth of equipment to obtain a sale. Whatever the situation, the communication seeks a response from the audience. You are trying to *persuade*.

But when does persuasion become manipulation? And what's the difference? I can see two cavemen with limited communication skills summarizing these concepts: "Persuasion . . . good! Manipulation . . . bad!"

In actuality, there's a fine line between these two concepts. Note the following signs that help you know which side of the line you're on and when you're crossing it:

Are you speaking the truth? If so, the likelihood you're manipulating an audience is low. You can still cross the line to get people to accept your message, but speaking only the truth helps keep you on the "good" side.

Are you acting in the interests of the audience or in your own self-interests? If you always act in the interests of your audience members, you can't be accused of manipulation. If their needs are met as well as yours, that's *very* "good."

Have you injected too much emotion into your presentation? Remember, rapport depends on making an initial emotional connection with the audience. Indeed, you should keep the emotional contact throughout your presentation if you can. But if the emotion becomes the primary source of the request for action, you've crossed the line into manipulation. "Bad." The formula, then, is this:

Emotion + logic + serving the best interests of the audience = persuasion = "good"

Communication in today's business world creates another paradox. With business complexities growing by the day, never has the need for simple, clear communication been so great. And yet, the state of communication skills is totally inadequate. Today, we hide behind jargon. We turn verbs into nouns, such as "Do you have a solve for this problem? Let's focus on the build. Can't action that right now" and so on, believing that makes us sound erudite. We're shrouded in corporate speak, such as claiming we're "increasing the viability of existing platforms while exploring new resources for enhanced consumer services." What does that mean?

In the public sphere, our politicians use their platforms as a means to evade the hard answers and push their own agendas while pandering to their own base constituents. Masters of manipulation, they use the bridge techniques to spin the underlying facts to suit their needs.

Sometime in your career, you'll be called on to face a crowd. When that time comes, focus on your listeners. Know their needs and wants. Use the concept of rapport to bond with them. Practice the techniques here so when you open your mouth, your words and ideas flow with ease and truth. And remember that in some way—even if it's small—whenever you give a speech, seminar, or presentation, you have the opportunity to change the world.

Seize that opportunity. Dare to Speak!

ABOUT THE AUTHORS

Frank M. Manfredi lectures to various business groups on results-oriented efforts and techniques. He conducts seminars for governmental agencies to "partner" contracts with general contractors. He is currently employed in the construction field.

Frank has published two books, *Essays on the Proper Path*, containing essays on the perplexities and paradoxes of life, and *For the Dreamers: Quotations from the Wise*, which focuses on historical sayings that still have meaning today.

Anthony F. Manfredi has been a leader in Enterprise Performance Management software space for more than 17 years. Today, he leads a global practice as a principal in the Hackett Group. He has conducted numerous presentations for clients, education events, and user conferences. Anthony was admitted to the New York State Bar as an attorney in 2006.

BIBLIOGRAPHY

Bartolome, Fernando. *The Articulate Executive: Orchestrating Effective Communication.* Boston, MA: Harvard Business School Press, 1993.

Bates, Suzanne. *Speak like a CEO: Secrets for Commanding Attention and Getting Results.* New York: McGraw-Hill, 2005.

Dempsey, David J. *Present Your Way to the Top.* New York: McGraw-Hill, 2010. [Hardcover and Kindle]

Dowis, Richard. *The Lost Art of the Great Speech: Everything You Need to Know to Write and Deliver a Great Speech.* New York: MJF Books, 2000.

Hoff, Ron. *I Can See You Naked: A New Revised Edition of the National Bestseller on Making Fearless Presentations.* Kansas City: Andrews and McMeel, 1992.

Jolles, Robert L. *How to Run Seminars and Workshops: Presentation Skills for Consultants, Trainers, and Teachers.* New York: John Wiley & Sons, 1993.

Morgan, Nick. *Give Your Speech, Change the World: How to Move Your Audience to Action.* Boston: Harvard Business School, 2005.

Noonan, Peggy. *Simply Speaking: How to Communicate Your Ideas with Style, Substance, and Clarity.* New York: Harper, 1998.

Spence, Gerry. *How to Argue and Win Every Time: At Home, at Work, in Court, Everywhere, Every Day.* New York: St. Martin's Press, 1995.

Wolfe. "Broadband Video Conferencing as Knowledge Management Tool." *Journal of Knowledge Management* 11 no 2, 2007.

Ferrin, Carlos, and Watts. "Video Conferencing in the field: a heuristic processing model." *Management Science* 54 no 9, 2007.

ENDNOTES

1   Peggy   Noonan,   *Simply   Speaking: How   to Communicate Your Ideas with Style, Substance, and Clarity.* New York: Harper, 1998. p. 12.

2   *Ibid,* p. 37.

3   *Ibid,* pp. 50-51.

4   William Shakespeare, *Hamlet* (3.2 1-36)